ALTO SAX

101 JAZZ SONGS

Available for
FLUTE, CLARINET, ALTO SAX, TENOR SAX, TRUMPET,
HORN, TROMBONE, VIOLIN, VIOLA, CELLO

ISBN 978-1-4950-2339-2

HAL•LEONARD®
CORPORATION

7777 W. BLUEMOUND RD. P.O. BOX 13819 MILWAUKEE, WI 53213

Visit Hal Leonard Online at
www.halleonard.com

CONTENTS

ALL OF ME

ALTO SAX

Words and Music by SEYMOUR SIMONS
and GERALD MARKS

Moderately

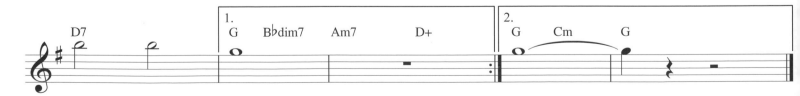

ALL THE THINGS YOU ARE

ALTO SAX

Lyrics by OSCAR HAMMERSTEIN II
Music by JEROME KERN

APRIL IN PARIS

ALTO SAX

Words by E.Y. "YIP" HARBURG
Music by VERNON DUKE

AUTUMN IN NEW YORK

ALTO SAX

Words and Music by
VERNON DUKE

AUTUMN LEAVES

ALTO SAX

English Lyric by JOHNNY MERCER
French Lyric by JACQUES PREVERT
Music by JOSEPH KOSMA

BEWITCHED

ALTO SAX

Words by LORENZ HART
Music by RICHARD RODGERS

BEYOND THE SEA

Lyrics by JACK LAWRENCE
Music by CHARLES TRENET and ALBERT LASRY
Original French Lyric to "La Mer" by CHARLES TRENET

ALTO SAX

THE BLUE ROOM

ALTO SAX

Words by LORENZ HART
Music by RICHARD RODGERS

BLUE SKIES

ALTO SAX

Words and Music by
IRVING BERLIN

BLUESETTE

ALTO SAX

Words by NORMAN GIMBEL
Music by JEAN THIELEMANS

BODY AND SOUL

ALTO SAX

Words by EDWARD HEYMAN,
ROBERT SOUR and FRANK EYTON
Music by JOHN GREEN

BUT BEAUTIFUL

ALTO SAX

Words by JOHNNY BURKE
Music by JIMMY VAN HEUSEN

CAN'T HELP LOVIN' DAT MAN

ALTO SAX

Lyrics by OSCAR HAMMERSTEIN II
Music by JEROME KERN

CARAVAN

ALTO SAX

Words and Music by DUKE ELLINGTON,
IRVING MILLS and JUAN TIZOL

CHARADE

ALTO SAX

By HENRY MANCINI

Medium Waltz

CHEEK TO CHEEK

ALTO SAX

Words and Music by
IRVING BERLIN

COME RAIN OR COME SHINE

ALTO SAX

Words by JOHNNY MERCER
Music by HAROLD ARLEN

Dancing on the Ceiling

ALTO SAX

Words by LORENZ HART
Music by RICHARD RODGERS

DEARLY BELOVED

ALTO SAX

Music by JEROME KERN
Words by JOHNNY MERCER

DO NOTHIN' TILL YOU HEAR FROM ME

ALTO SAX

Words and Music by DUKE ELLINGTON
and BOB RUSSELL

DON'T GET AROUND MUCH ANYMORE

ALTO SAX

Words and Music by DUKE ELLINGTON
and BOB RUSSELL

DREAMSVILLE

ALTO SAX

By Henry Mancini

FALLING IN LOVE WITH LOVE

ALTO SAX

Words by LORENZ HART
Music by RICHARD RODGERS

A FINE ROMANCE

ALTO SAX

Words by DOROTHY FIELDS
Music by JEROME KERN

FLY ME TO THE MOON
(In Other Words)

Alto Sax

Words and Music by
BART HOWARD

Georgia on My Mind

ALTO SAX

Words by STUART GORRELL
Music by HOAGY CARMICHAEL

HERE'S THAT RAINY DAY

ALTO SAX

Words by JOHNNY BURKE
Music by JIMMY VAN HEUSEN

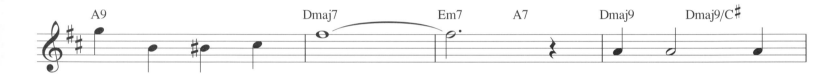

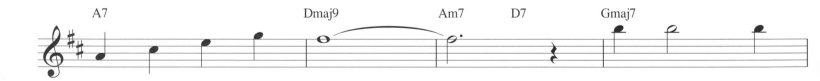

HERE'S TO LIFE

ALTO SAX

Music by ARTIE BUTLER
Lyrics by PHYLLIS MOLINARY

HONEYSUCKLE ROSE

ALTO SAX

Words by ANDY RAZAF
Music by THOMAS "FATS" WALLER

HOW DEEP IS THE OCEAN

(How High Is the Sky)

ALTO SAX

Words and Music by
IRVING BERLIN

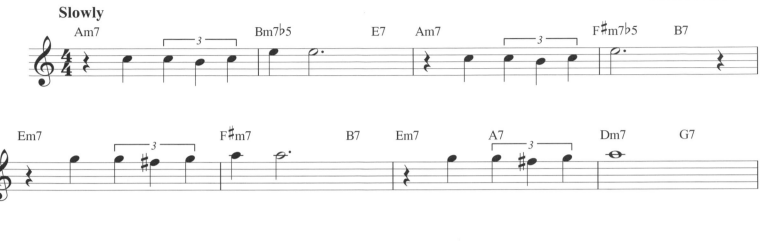

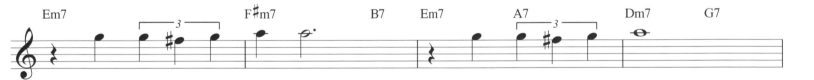

HOW INSENSITIVE
(Insensatez)

ALTO SAX

Music by ANTONIO CARLOS JOBIM
Original Words by VINICIUS DE MORAES
English Words by NORMAN GIMBEL

Medium Bossa Nova

I CAN'T GET STARTED

ALTO SAX

Words by IRA GERSHWIN
Music by VERNON DUKE

I COULD WRITE A BOOK

ALTO SAX

Words by LORENZ HART
Music by RICHARD RODGERS

I GOT IT BAD AND THAT AIN'T GOOD

ALTO SAX

Words by PAUL FRANCIS WEBSTER
Music by DUKE ELLINGTON

I'LL REMEMBER APRIL

ALTO SAX

Words and Music by PAT JOHNSTON,
DON RAYE AND GENE DE PAUL

I'M BEGINNING TO SEE THE LIGHT

Alto Sax

Words and Music by DON GEORGE, JOHNNY HODGES,
DUKE ELLINGTON and HARRY JAMES

Medium Bounce

I'VE GOT THE WORLD ON A STRING

ALTO SAX

Words by TED KOEHLER
Music by HAROLD ARLEN

IF I WERE A BELL

ALTO SAX

By FRANK LOESSER

Bright Swing

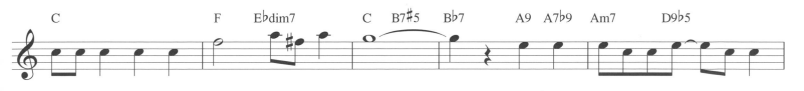

IMAGINATION

Alto Sax

Words by JOHNNY BURKE
Music by JIMMY VAN HEUSEN

Slowly, with a lilt

IN A SENTIMEMTAL MOOD

ALTO SAX

By DUKE ELLINGTON

IN THE WEE SMALL HOURS OF THE MORNING

ALTO SAX

Words by BOB HILLIARD
Music by DAVID MANN

INDIANA
(Back Home Again in Indiana)

ALTO SAX

Words by BALLARD MacDONALD
Music by JAMES F. HANLEY

ISN'T IT ROMANTIC?

ALTO SAX

Words by LORENZ HART
Music by RICHARD RODGERS

IT COULD HAPPEN TO YOU

ALTO SAX

Words by JOHNNY BURKE
Music by JAMES VAN HEUSEN

IT DON'T MEAN A THING

(If It Ain't Got That Swing)

ALTO SAX

Words and Music by DUKE ELLINGTON
and IRVING MILLS

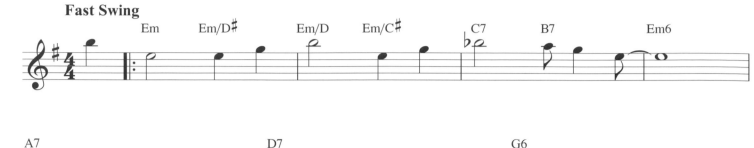

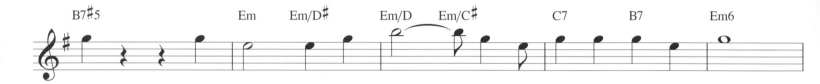

IT MIGHT AS WELL BE SPRING

ALTO SAX

Lyrics by OSCAR HAMMERSTEIN II
Music by RICHARD RODGERS

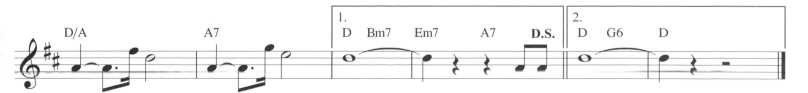

THE LADY IS A TRAMP

ALTO SAX

Words by LORENZ HART
Music by RICHARD RODGERS

LAZY RIVER

ALTO SAX

Words and Music by HOAGY CARMICHAEL
and SIDNEY ARODIN

LET THERE BE LOVE

ALTO SAX

Lyric by IAN GRANT
Music by LIONEL RAND

LIKE SOMEONE IN LOVE

ALTO SAX

Words by JOHNNY BURKE
Music by JIMMY VAN HEUSEN

LITTLE GIRL BLUE

ALTO SAX

Words by LORENZ HART
Music by RICHARD RODGERS

LONG AGO (AND FAR AWAY)

ALTO SAX

Words by IRA GERSHWIN
Music by JEROME KERN

LOVER, COME BACK TO ME

ALTO SAX

Lyrics by OSCAR HAMMERSTEIN II
Music by SIGMUND ROMBERG

LULLABY OF BIRDLAND

ALTO SAX

Words by GEORGE DAVID WEISS
Music by GEORGE SHEARING

Moderate Swing

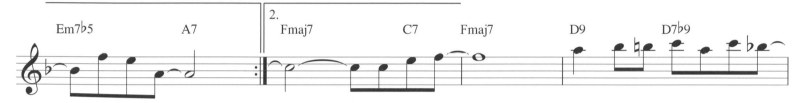

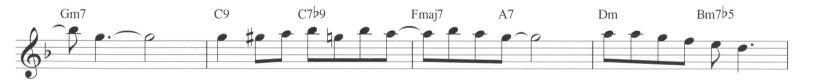

LULLABY OF THE LEAVES

ALTO SAX

Words by JOE YOUNG
Music by BERNICE PETKERE

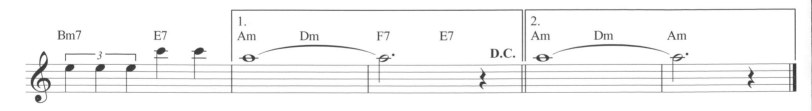

MANHATTAN

ALTO SAX

Words by LORENZ HART
Music by RICHARD RODGERS

MEDITATION
(Meditação)

ALTO SAX

Music by ANTONIO CARLOS JOBIM
Original Words by NEWTON MENDONÇA
English Words by NORMAN GIMBEL

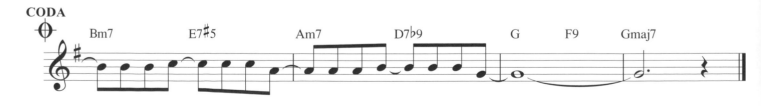

MIDNIGHT SUN

ALTO SAX

Words and Music by LIONEL HAMPTON,
SONNY BURKE and JOHNNY MERCER

MISTY

ALTO SAX

Music by ERROLL GARNER

Slowly, with a smooth Swing

MOOD INDIGO

ALTO SAX

Words and Music by DUKE ELLINGTON,
IRVING MILLS and ALBANY BIGARD

MOONLIGHT IN VERMONT

ALTO SAX

Words by JOHN BLACKBURN
Music by KARL SUESSDORF

MORE THAN YOU KNOW

ALTO SAX

Words by WILLIAM ROSE and EDWARD ELISCU
Music by VINCENT YOUMANS

Slowly, with expression

MY HEART STOOD STILL

ALTO SAX

Words by LORENZ HART
Music by RICHARD RODGERS

MY OLD FLAME

ALTO SAX

Words and Music by ARTHUR JOHNSTON
and SAM COSLOW

Moderate Swing

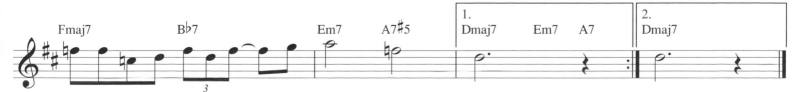

MY ONE AND ONLY LOVE

ALTO SAX

Words by ROBERT MELLIN
Music by GUY WOOD

MY ROMANCE

ALTO SAX

Words by LORENZ HART
Music by RICHARD RODGERS

MY SHIP

ALTO SAX

Words by IRA GERSHWIN
Music by KURT WEILL

THE NEARNESS OF YOU

ALTO SAX

Words by NED WASHINGTON
Music by HOAGY CARMICHAEL

A NIGHT IN TUNISIA

ALTO SAX

By JOHN "DIZZY" GILLESPIE
and FRANK PAPARELLI

Moderately fast Swing

ON GREEN DOLPHIN STREET

ALTO SAX

Lyrics by NED WASHINGTON
Music by BRONISLAU KAPER

Moderately

ONE NOTE SAMBA
(Samba de uma nota so)

Alto Sax

Original Lyrics by NEWTON MENDONÇA
English Lyrics by ANTONIO CARLOS JOBIM
Music by ANTONIO CARLOS JOBIM

Medium Bossa Nova

PICK YOURSELF UP

ALTO SAX

Words by DOROTHY FIELDS
Music by JEROME KERN

POLKA DOTS AND MOONBEAMS

Alto Sax

Words by JOHNNY BURKE
Music by JIMMY VAN HEUSEN

QUIET NIGHTS OF QUIET STARS

(Corcovado)

ALTO SAX

English Words by GENE LEES
Original Words and Music by ANTONIO CARLOS JOBIM

Medium Bossa Nova

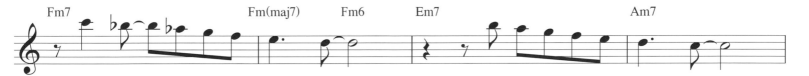

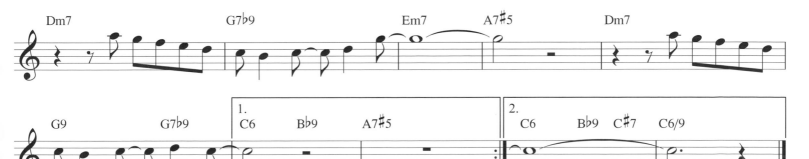

SATIN DOLL

ALTO SAX

By DUKE ELLINGTON

SKYLARK

ALTO SAX

Words by JOHNNY MERCER
Music by HOAGY CARMICHAEL

Moderate Swing

SO NICE
(Summer Samba)

ALTO SAX

Original Words and Music by MARCOS VALLE
and PAULO SERGIO VALLE
English Words by NORMAN GIMBEL

Medium Bossa Nova

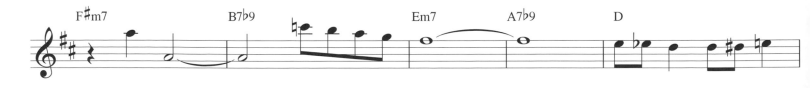

SOPHISTICATED LADY

Alto Sax

Words and Music by DUKE ELLINGTON,
IRVING MILLS and MITCHELL PARISH

SPEAK LOW

ALTO SAX

Words by OGDEN NASH
Music by KURT WEILL

STELLA BY STARLIGHT

ALTO SAX

Words by NED WASHINGTON
Music by VICTOR YOUNG

STOMPIN' AT THE SAVOY

ALTO SAX

By BENNY GOODMAN,
EDGAR SAMPSON and CHICK WEBB

Bright Swing

STORMY WEATHER
(Keeps Rainin' All the Time)

ALTO SAX

Lyric by TED KOEHLER
Music by HAROLD ARLEN

A SUNDAY KIND OF LOVE

ALTO SAX

Words and Music by LOUIS PRIMA, ANITA NYE LEONARD,
STANLEY RHODES and BARBARA BELLE

TANGERINE

ALTO SAX

Words by JOHNNY MERCER
Music by VICTOR SCHERTZINGER

THERE'S A SMALL HOTEL

ALTO SAX

Words by LORENZ HART
Music by RICHARD RODGERS

THESE FOOLISH THINGS (REMIND ME OF YOU)

ALTO SAX

Words by HOLT MARVELL
Music by JACK STRACHEY

THE THINGS WE DID LAST SUMMER

ALTO SAX

Words by SAMMY CAHN
Music by JULE STYNE

Moderate Swing

THIS CAN'T BE LOVE

ALTO SAX

Words by LORENZ HART
Music by RICHARD RODGERS

THOU SWELL

ALTO SAX

Words by LORENZ HART
Music by RICHARD RODGERS

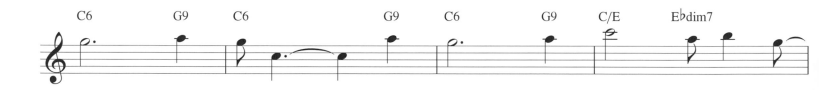

UNFORGETTABLE

ALTO SAX

Words and Music by
IRVING GORDON

THE VERY THOUGHT OF YOU

ALTO SAX

Words and Music by
RAY NOBLE

WATCH WHAT HAPPENS

Music by MICHEL LEGRAND
Original French Text by JACQUES DEMY
English Lyrics by NORMAN GIMBEL

ALTO SAX

Moderately

WAVE

ALTO SAX

Words and Music by
ANTONIO CARLOS JOBIM

Medium Bossa Nova

THE WAY YOU LOOK TONIGHT

Alto Sax

Words by DOROTHY FIELDS
Music by JEROME KERN

WHAT'LL I DO

ALTO SAX

Words and Music by
IRVING BERLIN

WILLOW WEEP FOR ME

ALTO SAX

Words and Music by
ANN RONELL

WITCHCRAFT

ALTO SAX

Music by CY COLEMAN
Lyrics by CAROLYN LEIGH

Moderately

YESTERDAYS

ALTO SAX

Words by OTTO HARBACH
Music by JEROME KERN

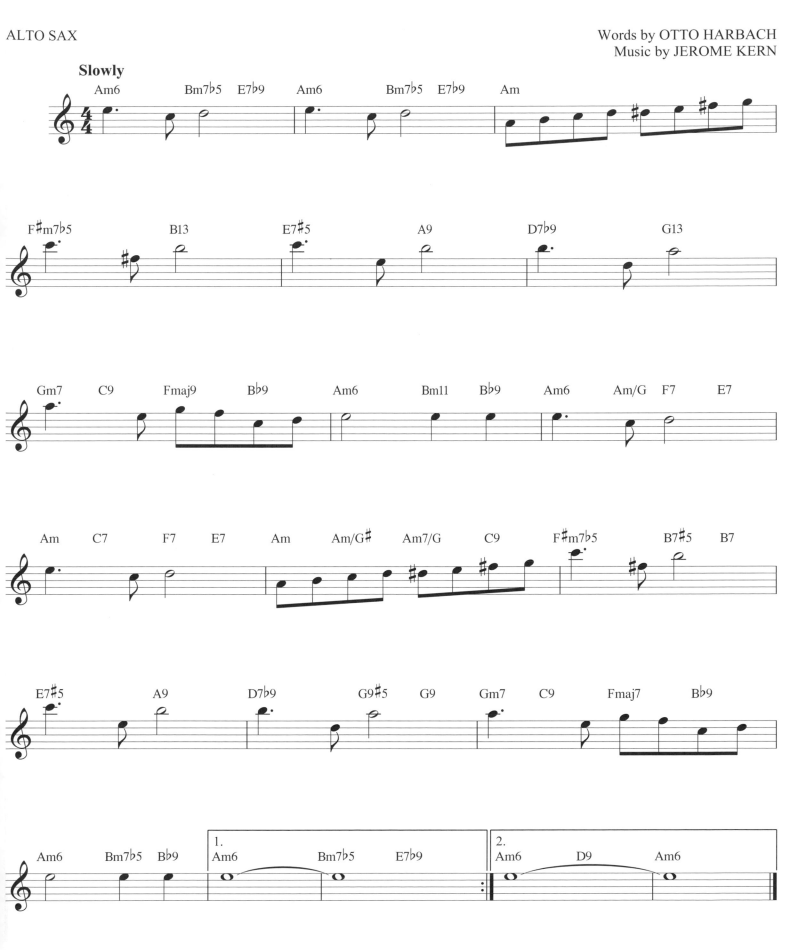

YOU ARE TOO BEAUTIFUL

ALTO SAX

Words by LORENZ HART
Music by RICHARD RODGERS

YOU BROUGHT A NEW KIND OF LOVE TO ME

Alto Sax

Words and Music by SAMMY FAIN,
IRVING KAHAL and PIERRE NORMAN

Medium Swing

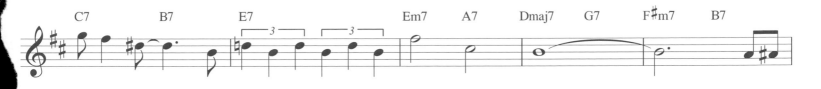

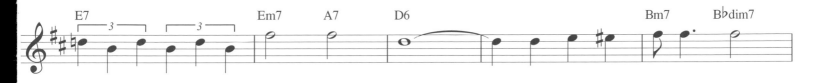

YOU DON'T KNOW WHAT LOVE IS

ALTO SAX

Words and Music by DON RAYE
and GENE DePAUL